CRITICAL THINKING
ACTIVITIES TO IM
WRITING SKILLS

D1648334

Whatcha-Macallits A1

—Books in this series—
Descriptive Mysteries
Where-Abouts
Arguments
Whatcha-Macallits

Michael Baker • Gaeir Dietrich
Elizabeth Korver • Bonnie Baker

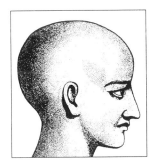

© 1991
CRITICAL THINKING BOOKS & SOFTWARE
www.criticalthinking.com
P.O. Box 448 • Pacific Grove • CA 93950-0448
Phone 800-458-4849 • FAX 831-393-3277
ISBN 0-89455-388-7
Printed in the United States of America

Teaching Suggestions

ABOUT THIS SERIES

The books in this series provide teachers with easy-to-use critical thinking activities that emphasize real-life communication skills.

ABOUT THIS BOOK

Students are asked to identify the characteristics of a given set of objects and to communicate the information to other students in written form. The written information should be clear enough to allow the reader to name or draw a member of the set described by the writer. Any answer the writer can logically support is acceptable. Students should always be asked to explain how they arrived at their answers. Some of the activities in this book are illustrated and some are not. Illustrations have nothing to do with degree of difficulty. The activities spiral up in difficulty as you progress through each section of the book.

PURPOSE

1. To help students develop the skills of expressing themselves precisely and concisely in writing, and to learn the importance of including complete and accurate detail when communicating with others in writing.

2. To teach students to recognize patterns and similar and dissimilar attributes that aid them in classifying.

3. To help students distinguish between relevant and irrelevant information.

4. To increase students' abilities in associative reasoning, divergent thinking, and evaluative skills.

OBJECTIVES

1. Given a group of illustrations and/or several *positive, negative, or possibility* statements, a student will examine each item for its attributes. The student will identify common attributes and attributes that are different.

2. Using these attributes the student will look for patterns that allow him or her to identify the characteristics of the set which has been given a "nonsense" name.

3. The student will then write a precise description of the set so that another student, after reading only that description, will be able to name or draw a member of the set and explain why the item is a member of that set.

PROCEDURE

1. The teacher should first divide the class into small groups. Call half of the groups Group 1s and the other half Group 2s. (Students may also work in pairs instead. In this case the two students would be named students 1 and 2.)

2. The teacher should select two Whatcha–Macallits activities and make enough copies so that Group 1s get one activity and Group 2s get the second activity.

3. Students in Group 1 should not show their activity to anyone in Group 2 and vice versa. Students working together on the same Whatcha–Macallit can quietly exchange information to solve the problem and write their definition.

4. The students should study the illustrations or statements about what is or is not a member of the set they are trying to identify. They should try to figure out all the attributes the items have in common and then look at any differences so they can tell what specific attributes allow the items to belong to the set and which attributes keep them from belonging to the set.

5. Students should have access to reference materials so they can look up information about items that are not familiar to them.

6. When they are finished writing definitions, Groups 1 and 2 should exchange their writing sheets—not the activity sheets.

7. Students should then read each others definitions and try to name or draw an item that would have the attributes given in the definition that would allow it to fit into the named set.

8. Groups 1 and 2 should then check their answers with the teacher. **Any answer that students can correctly support is acceptable.**

9. If a group gave the wrong definition, the answer given by the exchange group will not be correct either (even though if will fit the definition) and the activity will have to be done over by both groups. It may also be helpful at this time to have students discuss why their thinking processes did or did not work with this activity.

EXTENDING ACTIVITIES

1. Explain why the other items shown do not fit into the set. Describe how their attributes are different and keep them from belonging to the set.

2. In some of the verbal activities, an item is described with the qualifier *can, sometimes, or may be.* Explain how that item may be a member of a set in one situation and not in another.

Answers

Page

Introductory

5. A **Bentor** is an object designed to be sat on.
6. A **Tufutu** is something worn on the feet.
7. A **Hebfin** is an object used for drawing (or for putting colored marks on paper.)
8. A **Scruggy** is an animal that has many legs and is long and narrow in shape.
   A **Lembone** is a unit of metric measurement.
9. A **Merent** is something usually found in a bedroom.
10. A **Hargraw** is used to hold things together.

Mixed Bag

11. A **Fliger** is an object designed to drink from.
12. A **Rinrin** is a boat which does not need a motor to move.
13. A **Nimrad** is a reference book.
    A **Wogin** is an object that is worn on the head.
14. A **Lish** is an object designed to hold water or other fluids.
    An **Edfat** is a structure designed primarily as a storage place.
15. A **Mumbly** is a food that is round in shape with a hole in the middle.
    A **Clapwok** is something that holds things together without putting a hole in it.
16. A **Sizit** is a low, soft sound.
    A **Slithnod** is a liquid that is safe to drink.
17. A **Zoboe** is a clown dressed like someone who works in a real profession.
18. A **Regnad** is a sign that warns of danger. (Smoking is hazardous to your health but a "no smoking" sign just indicates smoking is not allowed in this area.)
19. A **Dolump** is a vessel suitable for serving food at the table.
    A **Botz** is a musical instrument that you need to strike in order to get musical sound from it.
20. A **Limpa** is an animal that has just two legs.
    An **Ortsa** is a zodiac sign represented by an animal that has horns.
21. A **Penma** is a monster that has two eyes, teeth or fangs, two legs, and hair.
22. A **Serp** is part of a speech made by a U.S. president.
23. A **Zig** is an object that has a horizontal line drawn through its center.
24. A **Magnot** is a rectangle around a square that encloses a circle which touches the top of the square.

Page

25. A **Berta** is a sequence of three or more objects of the same shape that are reduced in size from left to right.
26. A **Murlap** is a group of two or more objects each of which intersect with at least one of the other objects in the group.

Mathematics

27. A **Flimbot** is a figure (equilateral polygon) with equal-length sides.
28. A **Grizwik** is a figure (equiangular and equilateral polygon) with equal sides and equal angles.
29. A **Nintel** is a polygon containing at least one right angle.
30. A **Kwert** is a polygon that is made up of line segments that only meet at their end points.
31. A **Durwit** is a figure (quadrilateral) that has four sides.
32. A **Kurzla** is a four-sided figure (parallelogram) with the opposite sides parallel.

Science

33. A **Snigin** is a water bird that has webbed feet, a broad bill, and swims (duck family).
34. An **Edmag** is a fish that lives in the ocean.
    A **Zibber** is a naturally occurring source of energy.
35. A **Rifer** is a bird that does not fly.
36. A **Reevig** is a mammal that spends most of its time in trees.
37. A **Dingbow** is something that is propelled by wind.
    A **Mootentooten** is an animal that lays eggs to produce its young.
38. A **Tocktee** is a tool used to measure time or distance.
    A **Gugbug** is an animal that raises its young in a burrow.
39. A **Fiznor** is a storm that carries high winds and heavy rain.
    A **Sleeco** is a vegetable that is green and has a long narrow shape.
40. A **Grelcer** is a tree with needles and cones that does not loose its leaves in the winter (evergreen conifers).
    An **Unch** is a food that makes a loud crunchy sound when you eat it.
41. A **Xick** is an animal that flies and has a name that begins with B.

©1991 CRITICAL THINKING PRESS & SOFTWARE • P.O. Box 448, Pacific Grove, CA 93950

Answers

Page

42. A **Plasmoid** is a planet with three or more moons.

43. A **Gwig** is an animal that changes its coat color with summer and winter.
A **Lolly** is a measurement of quantity based on the volume of the container.

44. A **Vethig** is a mammal that has a fairly long neck, splayed feet, a cleft upper lip, and is medium to large (members of the camel family).

45. A **Dref** is a nonextinct animal that glides through the air but does not actually fly.

Page

46. A **Prentga** is a fresh-water bird that eats fish.

Geography

47. A **Wirtnee** is a country that has an Atlantic coastline.

48. A **Ravsic** is a country that has part of its land mass within the Arctic Circle.

49. A **Vober** is a country in Africa through which the Nile River flows.

50. A **Zimmer** is a country or continent that has both an Atlantic and a Pacific coastline.

Table of Contents

GUIDED PRACTICE

Hand out a copy of the Sample Activities on page 3 to each student or make a transparency for the overhead.

Go through the 2 activities with the total class so they understand the objectives of the lessons.

Sample Activity 1 (on page 3) is a fairly simple activity. After students have examined each item, they should be able to determine that all the items named as Beewees are fruits.

But strawberries are fruits too, so why aren't they Beewees? What attributes do strawberries have (or not have) that keep them from belonging to the set Beewees?

The teacher can help students by asking some of the following questions:

What do we know about these items?
What does each item look like?
What is its size?
What shape does it have?
What is its structure? What parts does it have?
What is it used for?
Where is it usually found?
How does it grow or where was it made?
What does it do?
What sounds does it make?
What is unusual about its behavior or means of locomotion?
Does it have any odor or a particular texture?
How does it make us feel and why does it make us feel that way?

Now .... What common factors or similarities are we finding?
What factor(s) differentiates an item from others on the list?

By asking these kinds of questions, students should be able to conclude that—

Beewees are fruits that have a pit in their center.

—and this could be the definition they would write. If students received this kind of written definition they could then respond by naming any fruit they can think of with a pit in its center, such as an avocado.

Sample Activity 2 is more complex. After examining each statement and looking at the illustrations, students should recognize that all Klicats

–are animals
–have hair
–have hooved feet
–have tails
–are mammals
–have manes on the backs of their necks

But they should also note that pigs, cows, and oxen have most of these things also. So what attributes keep them from being Klicats?

After examining all the common and different attributes of each item, students should eventually arrive at the conclusion that having a mane on its neck is the prime attribute that separates Klicats from other items on the list. Students would then write the definition—

A Klicat has a mane on its neck.

This short definition is concise and sufficient and would leave the set open to many other members. The group receiving the definition could respond with—

A giraffe is a Klicat.

If students want to close the set more, they can add just some or all of the other attributes noted above. If a group decides to use all of them, the responding group could answer with—

A giraffe would be a member of the set, Klicats,
because a giraffe is a mammal with hair, hooves,
a tail, and a mane on its neck.

Encourage students to write in complete sentences and to use proper punctuation and grammar. Teachers should accept answers with attributes in any order, and any answers that students can reasonably support. Encourage students to experiment with different sentence patterns.

A student work sheet master is provided on page 4.

©1991 CRITICAL THINKING PRESS & SOFTWARE • P.O. Box 448, Pacific Grove, CA 93950

STUDENT PRACTICE PAGE

Sample Activity 1

Peaches are Beewees.   **Peas are not Beewees.**

Carrots are not Beewees.   **Plums are Beewees.**

Cherries are Beewees.   **Spinach leaves are not Beewees.**

Strawberries are not Beewees.

Sample Activity 2

A horse is a Klicat.

An ox is not a Klicat.

A pig is not a Klicat.

A cow is not a Klicat.

A bison is a Klicat.

A zebra is a Klicat.

STUDENT WORK SHEET

Student 1 or Group 1:

Name the set and write the characteristics of the set.

Set Name:_____

Characteristics of Members:
1.
2.
3.
4.
5.
6.

 Write a complete description of the set using all the relevant attributes and as much fine detail as possible. Write in complete sentences and use proper grammar and punctuation.

_____

_____

_____

_____

_____

Student 2 or Group 2:

Name or draw a member of this set.

Bentors

Look at the objects in the set called Bentors. What attributes do they have in common that makes them members of this set? Using complete sentences, describe these attributes so that someone reading your description could name or draw a member of the same set. Keep in mind that there may be more Bentors than just the ones you see below. When you are finished, give the description to your partner. S/he will then name or draw a member of the set Bentors.

A chair is a Bentor.

A desk is not a Bentor.

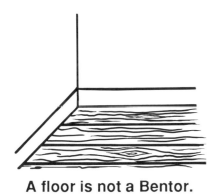

A floor is not a Bentor.

A table is not a Bentor.

A couch is a Bentor.

A stool is a Bentor.

Tufutus

Look at the objects in the set called Tufutus. What attributes do they have in common that makes them members of this set? Using complete sentences, describe these attributes so that someone reading your description could name or draw a member of the same set. Keep in mind that there may be more Tufutus than just the ones you see below. When you are finished, give the description to your partner. S/he will then name or draw a member of the set Tufutus.

A sock is a Tufutu.

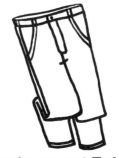

Pants are not Tufutus.

Gloves are not Tufutus.

A hat is not a Tufutu.

Shoes are Tufutus.

Slippers are Tufutus.

Hebfins

Look at the objects in the set called Hebfins. What attributes do they have in common that makes them members of this set? Using complete sentences, describe these attributes so that someone reading your description could name or draw a member of the same set. Keep in mind that there may be more Hebfins than just the ones you see below. When you are finished, give the description to your partner. S/he will then name or draw a member of the set Hebfins.

A paintbrush is a Hebfin.

A shoe brush is not a Hebfin.

A pin is not a Hebfin.

Scissors are not a Hebfin.

A colored marker is a Hebfin.

A crayon is a Hebfin.

Scruggies

Look at the objects in the set called Scruggies. What attributes do they have in common that makes them members of this set? Using complete sentences, describe these attributes so that someone reading your description could name or draw a member of the same set. Keep in mind that there may be more Scruggies than just the ones you see below. When you are finished, give the description to your partner. S/he will then name or draw a member of the set Scruggies.

A caterpillar is a Scruggy.   **A spider is not a Scruggy.**

A housefly is not a Scruggy.   **A millipede is a Scruggy.**

A centipede is a Scruggy.   **A ladybug is not a Scruggy.**

Lembones

Look at the objects in the set called Lembones. What attributes do they have in common that makes them members of this set? Using complete sentences, describe these attributes so that someone reading your description could name or draw a member of the same set. Keep in mind that there may be more Lembones than just the ones you see below. When you are finished, give the description to your partner. S/he will then name or draw a member of the set Lembones.

An inch is not a Lembone.   **A liter is a Lembone.**

A centimeter is a Lembone.   **A mile is not a Lembone.**

A ton is not a Lembone.   **A kilogram is a Lembone.**

Merents

Look at the objects in the set called Merents. What attributes do they have in common that makes them members of this set? Using complete sentences, describe these attributes so that someone reading your description could name or draw a member of the same set. Keep in mind that there may be more Merents than just the ones you see below. When you are finished, give the description to your partner. S/he will then name or draw a member of the set Merents.

A bed is a Merent.

A washing machine is not a Merent.

A stove is not a Merent.

A sink is not a Merent.

A closet is a Merent.

A dresser is a Merent.

Hargraws

Look at the objects in the set called Hargraws. What attributes do they have in common that makes them members of this set? Using complete sentences, describe these attributes so that someone reading your description could name or draw a member of the same set. Keep in mind that there may be more Hargraws than just the ones you see below. When you are finished, give the description to your partner. S/he will then name or draw a member of the set Hargraws.

A nail is a Hargraw.

A ruler is not a Hargraw.

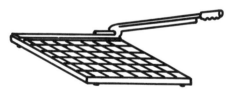

A paper cutter is not a Hargraw.

A wrench is not a Hargraw.

A screw is a Hargraw.

Glue is a Hargraw.

Fligers

Look at the objects in the set called Fligers. What attributes do they have in common that makes them members of this set? Using complete sentences, describe these attributes so that someone reading your description could name or draw a member of the same set. Keep in mind that there may be more Fligers than just the ones you see below. When you are finished, give the description to your partner. S/he will then name or draw a member of the set Fligers.

A cup is a Fliger.

A fork is not a Fliger.

A pitcher is not a Fliger.

A saucer is not a Fliger.

A mug is a Fliger.

A glass is a Fliger.

Rinrins

Look at the objects in the set called Rinrins. What attributes do they have in common that makes them members of this set? Using complete sentences, describe these attributes so that someone reading your description could name or draw a member of the same set. Keep in mind that there may be more Rinrins than just the ones you see below. When you are finished, give the description to your partner. S/he will then name or draw a member of the set Rinrins.

A sailboat is a Rinrin.

A speedboat is not a Rinrin.

A steamship is not a Rinrin.

A tugboat is not a Rinrin.

A kayak is a Rinrin.

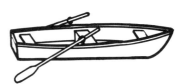

A rowboat is a Rinrin.

Nimrads

Look at the objects in the set called Nimrads. What attributes do they have in common that makes them members of this set? Using complete sentences, describe these attributes so that someone reading your description could name or draw a member of the same set. Keep in mind that there may be more Nimrads than just the ones you see below. When you are finished, give the description to your partner. S/he will then name or draw a member of the set Nimrads.

A dictionary is a Nimrad.   **A comic book is not a Nimrad.**

A novel is not a Nimrad.   **An encyclopedia is a Nimrad.**

An atlas is a Nimrad.   **A road map is not a Nimrad.**

Wogins

Look at the objects in the set called Wogins. What attributes do they have in common that makes them members of this set? Using complete sentences, describe these attributes so that someone reading your description could name or draw a member of the same set. Keep in mind that there may be more Wogins than just the ones you see below. When you are finished, give the description to your partner. S/he will then name or draw a member of the set Wogins.

A pair of eyeglasses is a Wogin.   **A shirt is not a Wogin.**

A pair of socks is not a Wogin.   **An earring is a Wogin.**

A hat is a Wogin.   **A necklace is not a Wogin.**

Lishes

Look at the objects in the set called Lishes. What attributes do they have in common that makes them members of this set? Using complete sentences, describe these attributes so that someone reading your description could name or draw a member of the same set. Keep in mind that there may be more Lishes than just the ones you see below. When you are finished, give the description to your partner. S/he will then name or draw a member of the set Lishes.

A tumbler is a Lish.

A knife is not a Lish.

A plate is not a Lish.

A vase is a Lish.

A cup is a Lish.

A strainer is not a Lish.

A shovel is not a Lish.

A pail is a Lish.

Edfats

Look at the objects in the set called Edfats. What attributes do they have in common that makes them members of this set? Using complete sentences, describe these attributes so that someone reading your description could name or draw a member of the same set. Keep in mind that there may be more Edfats than just the ones you see below. When you are finished, give the description to your partner. S/he will then name or draw a member of the set Edfats.

A silo is an Edfat.

A garage is an Edfat.

A hallway is not an Edfat.

A shed is an Edfat.

An attic is an Edfat.

A bathroom is not an Edfat.

A pool is not an Edfat.

A warehouse is an Edfat.

Mumblies

Look at the objects in the set called Mumblies. What attributes do they have in common that makes them members of this set? Using complete sentences, describe these attributes so that someone reading your description could name or draw a member of the same set. Keep in mind that there may be more Mumblies than just the ones you see below. When you are finished, give the description to your partner. S/he will then name or draw a member of the set Mumblies.

A doughnut is a Mumbly.

A bracelet is not a Mumbly.

A wedding ring is not a Mumbly.

An angel food cake usually is a Mumbly.

A coffee cake ring is a Mumbly

A spare tire is not a Mumbly.

A Lifesaver® is a Mumbly.

A gelatin ring is a Mumbly.

A hoop is not a Mumbly

Clapwoks

Look at the objects in the set called Clapwoks. What attributes do they have in common that makes them members of this set? Using complete sentences, describe these attributes so that someone reading your description could name or draw a member of the same set. Keep in mind that there may be more Clapwoks than just the ones you see below. When you are finished, give the description to your partner. S/he will then name or draw a member of the set Clapwoks.

A paper clip is a Clapwok.

A safety pin is not a Clapwok.

A nail is not a Clapwok.

A barrette is a Clapwok.

A vise is a Clapwok.

A staple is not a Clapwok.

A hatpin is not a Clapwok.

A rubber band is a Clapwok.

A paperweight is a Clapwok.

A tie pin is not a Clapwok.

A clamp is a Clapwok.

A tie clip is a Clapwok.

Sizits

Look at the objects in the set called Sizits. What attributes do they have in common that makes them members of this set? Using complete sentences, describe these attributes so that someone reading your description could name or draw a member of the same set. Keep in mind that there may be more Sizits than just the ones you see below. When you are finished, give the description to your partner. S/he will then name or draw a member of the set Sizits.

A whisper is a Sizit.   **A murmur is a Sizit.**

A cackle is not a Sizit.   **A roar is not a Sizit.**

A sigh is a Sizit.   **A mutter is a Sizit.**

A screech is not a Sizit.   **A scream is not a Sizit.**

A chuckle is a Sizit   **A hiss is a Sizit.**

A yell is not a Sizit.   **A holler is not a Sizit.**

Slithnods

Look at the objects in the set called Slithnods. What attributes do they have in common that makes them members of this set? Using complete sentences, describe these attributes so that someone reading your description could name or draw a member of the same set. Keep in mind that there may be more Slithnods than just the ones you see below. When you are finished, give the description to your partner. S/he will then name or draw a member of the set Slithnods.

Soda is a Slithnod.   **A cookie is not a Slithnod.**

Shampoo is not a Slithnod.   **Sea water is not a Slithnod.**

Water is a Slithnod.   **Lemonade is a Slithnod.**

Zoboes

Look at the objects in the set called Zoboes. What attributes do they have in common that makes them members of this set? Using complete sentences, describe these attributes so that someone reading your description could name or draw a member of the same set. Keep in mind that there may be more Zoboes than just the ones you see below. When you are finished, give the description to your partner. S/he will then name or draw a member of the set Zoboes.

This is a Zoboe.

This is not a Zoboe.

This is not a Zoboe.

This is a Zoboe.

This is a Zoboe.

This is not a Zoboe.

Regnads

Look at the objects in the set called Regnads. What attributes do they have in common that makes them members of this set? Using complete sentences, describe these attributes so that someone reading your description could name or draw a member of the same set. Keep in mind that there may be more Regnads than just the ones you see below. When you are finished, give the description to your partner. S/he will then name or draw a member of the set Regnads.

FLAMMABLE

This is a Regnad.

FIRST AID

This is not a Regnad.

NO SMOKING

This is not a Regnad.

POISON

This is a Regnad.

SLIPPERY FLOOR

This is a Regnad.

FIRE EXTINGUISHER

This is not a Regnad.

Dolumps

Look at the objects in the set called Dolumps. What attributes do they have in common that makes them members of this set? Using complete sentences, describe these attributes so that someone reading your description could name or draw a member of the same set. Keep in mind that there may be more Dolumps than just the ones you see below. When you are finished, give the description to your partner. S/he will then name or draw a member of the set Dolumps.

A platter is a Dolump.	**A scrub pail is not a Dolump.**
A sieve is not a Dolump.	**A burlap bag is not a Dolump.**
A bowl is a Dolump.	**A pan can be a Dolump.**
A skillet is not usually a Dolump.	**A plate is a Dolump.**
A tray is a Dolump.	**A basket can be a Dolump.**
A grill is not a Dolump.	

Botzes

Look at the objects in the set called Botzes. What attributes do they have in common that makes them members of this set? Using complete sentences, describe these attributes so that someone reading your description could name or draw a member of the same set. Keep in mind that there may be more Botzes than just the ones you see below. When you are finished, give the description to your partner. S/he will then name or draw a member of the set Botzes.

A bell is a Botz.	**A piano is a Botz.**
A violin is not a Botz.	**A tuba is not a Botz.**
A xylophone is a Botz.	**A slide trombone is not a Botz.**
A flute is not a Botz.	**A cymbal is a Botz.**
A triangle is a Botz.	**A harp is not a Botz.**

Limpas

Look at the objects in the set called Limpas. What attributes do they have in common that makes them members of this set? Using complete sentences, describe these attributes so that someone reading your description could name or draw a member of the same set. Keep in mind that there may be more Limpas than just the ones you see below. When you are finished, give the description to your partner. S/he will then name or draw a member of the set Limpas.

A human is a Limpa.   **A bear is not a Limpa.**

A spider is not a Limpa.   **An ape is a Limpa.**

A bird is a Limpa.   **A snake is not a Limpa.**

Ortsas

Look at the objects in the set called Ortsas. What attributes do they have in common that makes them members of this set? Using complete sentences, describe these attributes so that someone reading your description could name or draw a member of the same set. Keep in mind that there may be more Ortsas than just the ones you see below. When you are finished, give the description to your partner. S/he will then name or draw a member of the set Ortsas.

Aries is an Ortsa.   **Cancer is not an Ortsa.**

Leo is not an Ortsa.   **Taurus is an Ortsa.**

Capricorn is an Ortsa.   **Pisces is not an Ortsa.**

Penmas

Look at the objects in the set called Penmas. What attributes do they have in common that makes them members of this set? Using complete sentences, describe these attributes so that someone reading your description could name or draw a member of the same set. Keep in mind that there may be more Penmas than just the ones you see below. When you are finished, give the description to your partner. S/he will then name or draw a member of the set Penmas.

This is a Penma.

This is not a Penma.

This is not a Penma.

This is a Penma.

This is a Penma.

This is not a Penma.

Serps

Look at the objects in the set called Serps. What attributes do they have in common that makes them members of this set? Using complete sentences, describe these attributes so that someone reading your description could name or draw a member of the same set. Keep in mind that there may be more Serps than just the ones you see below. When you are finished, give the description to your partner. S/he will then name or draw a member of the set Serps.

This is a Serp.

"Ask not what your country can do for you, ask what you can do for your country."

This is not a Serp.

"I know not what course others may take, but as for me, give me liberty or give me death."

This is not a Serp.

"I have a dream that one day this nation will rise up and live out the true meaning of its creed."

This is not a Serp.

"Never in the field of human conflict was so much owed by so many to so few."

This is a Serp.

"This day will live in infamy."

This is a Serp.

"Fourscore and seven years ago, our forefathers brought forth upon this continent a new nation…"

Zigs

Look at the objects in the set called Zigs. What attributes do they have in common that makes them members of this set? Using complete sentences, describe these attributes so that someone reading your description could name or draw a member of the same set. Keep in mind that there may be more Zigs than just the ones you see below. When you are finished, give the description to your partner. S/he will then name or draw a member of the set Zigs.

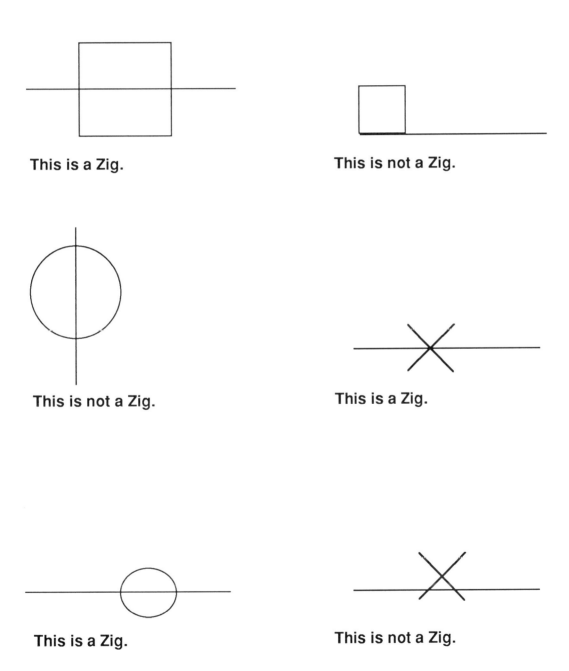

This is a Zig.   This is not a Zig.

This is not a Zig.   This is a Zig.

This is a Zig.   This is not a Zig.

Magnots

Look at the objects in the set called Magnots. What attributes do they have in common that makes them members of this set? Using complete sentences, describe these attributes so that someone reading your description could name or draw a member of the same set. Keep in mind that there may be more Magnots than just the ones you see below. When you are finished, give the description to your partner. S/he will then name or draw a member of the set Magnots.

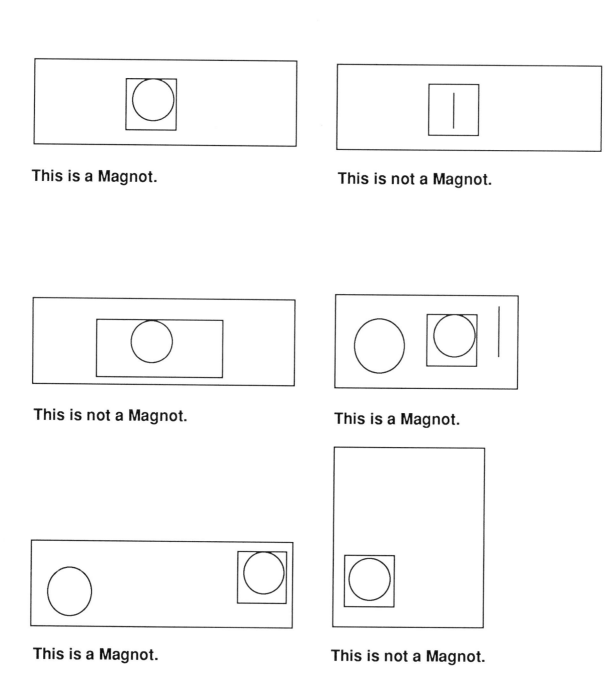

This is a Magnot.   This is not a Magnot.

This is not a Magnot.   This is a Magnot.

This is a Magnot.   This is not a Magnot.

Bertas

Look at the objects in the set called Bertas. What attributes do they have in common that makes them members of this set? Using complete sentences, describe these attributes so that someone reading your description could name or draw a member of the same set. Keep in mind that there may be more Bertas than just the ones you see below. When you are finished, give the description to your partner. S/he will then name or draw a member of the set Bertas.

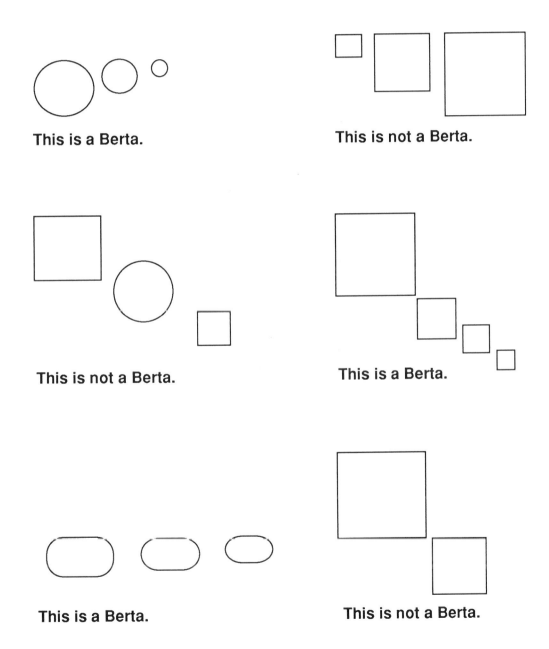

This is a Berta.

This is not a Berta.

This is not a Berta.

This is a Berta.

This is a Berta.

This is not a Berta.

Murlaps

Look at the objects in the set called Murlaps. What attributes do they have in common that makes them members of this set? Using complete sentences, describe these attributes so that someone reading your description could name or draw a member of the same set. Keep in mind that there may be more Murlaps than just the ones you see below. When you are finished, give the description to your partner. S/he will then name or draw a member of the set Murlaps.

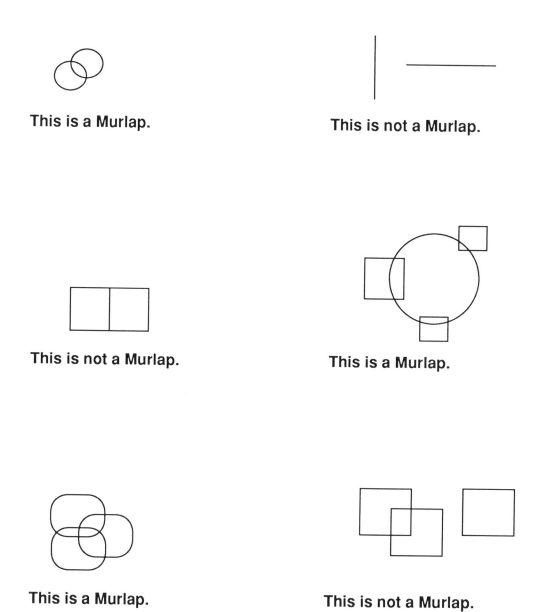

This is a Murlap.

This is not a Murlap.

This is not a Murlap.

This is a Murlap.

This is a Murlap.

This is not a Murlap.

Flimbots

Look at the objects in the set called Flimbots. What attributes do they have in common that makes them members of this set? Using complete sentences, describe these attributes so that someone reading your description could name or draw a member of the same set. Keep in mind that there may be more Flimbots than just the ones you see below. When you are finished, give the description to your partner. S/he will then name or draw a member of the set Flimbots.

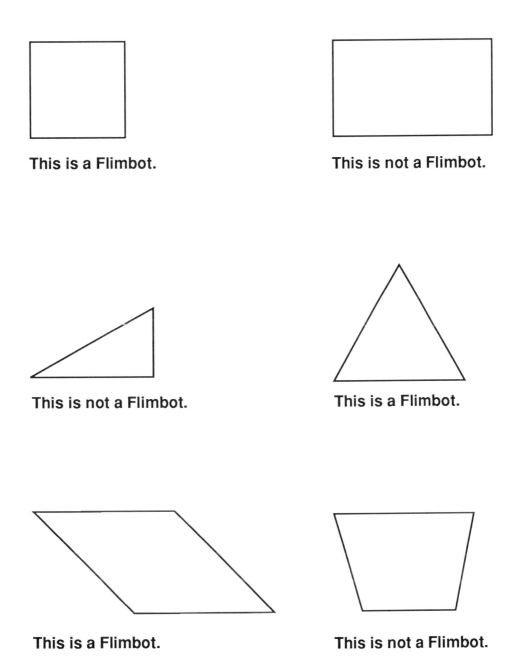

This is a Flimbot.   This is not a Flimbot.

This is not a Flimbot.   This is a Flimbot.

This is a Flimbot.   This is not a Flimbot.

Grizwiks

Look at the objects in the set called Grizwiks. What attributes do they have in common that makes them members of this set? Using complete sentences, describe these attributes so that someone reading your description could name or draw a member of the same set. Keep in mind that there may be more Grizwiks than just the ones you see below. When you are finished, give the description to your partner. S/he will then name or draw a member of the set Grizwiks.

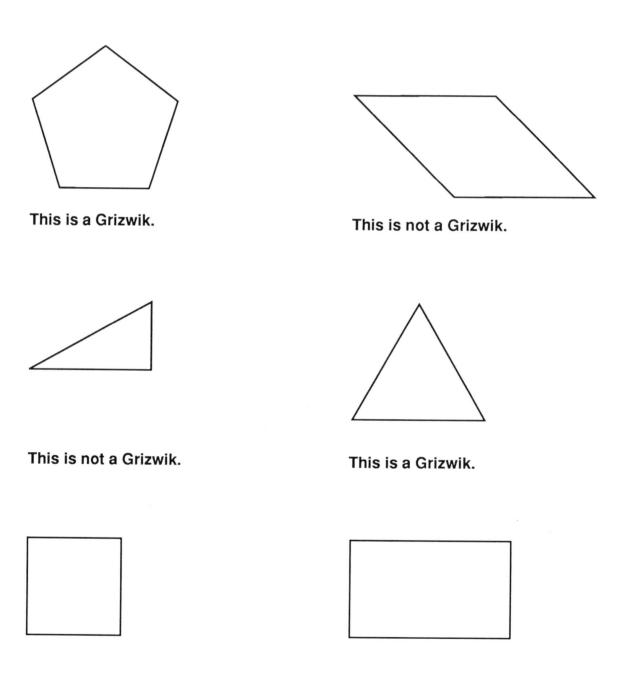

This is a Grizwik.

This is not a Grizwik.

This is not a Grizwik.

This is a Grizwik.

This is a Grizwik.

This is not a Grizwik.

Nintels

Look at the objects in the set called Nintels. What attributes do they have in common that makes them members of this set? Using complete sentences, describe these attributes so that someone reading your description could name or draw a member of the same set. Keep in mind that there may be more Nintels than just the ones you see below. When you are finished, give the description to your partner. S/he will then name or draw a member of the set Nintels.

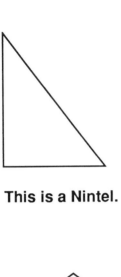

This is a Nintel.

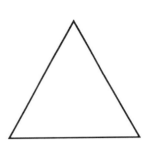

This is not a Nintel.

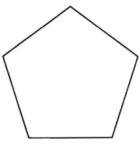

This is not a Nintel.

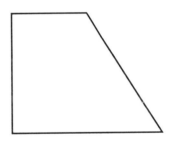

This is a Nintel.

This is a Nintel.

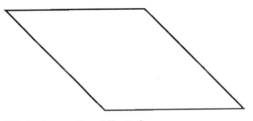

This is not a Nintel.

Kwerts

Look at the objects in the set called Kwerts. What attributes do they have in common that makes them members of this set? Using complete sentences, describe these attributes so that someone reading your description could name or draw a member of the same set. Keep in mind that there may be more Kwerts than just the ones you see below. When you are finished, give the description to your partner. S/he will then name or draw a member of the set Kwerts.

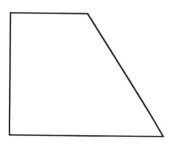

This is a Kwert.

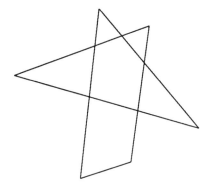

This is not a Kwert.

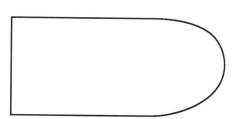

This is not a Kwert.

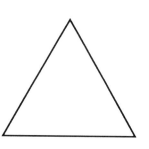

This is a Kwert.

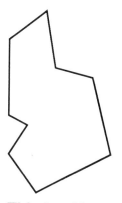

This is a Kwert.

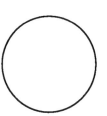

This is not a Kwert.

Durwits

Look at the objects in the set called Durwits. What attributes do they have in common that makes them members of this set? Using complete sentences, describe these attributes so that someone reading your description could name or draw a member of the same set. Keep in mind that there may be more Durwits than just the ones you see below. When you are finished, give the description to your partner. S/he will then name or draw a member of the set Durwits.

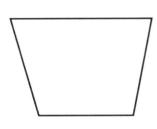

This is a Durwit.

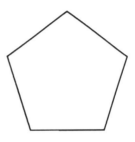

This is not a Durwit.

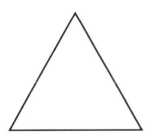

This is not a Durwit.

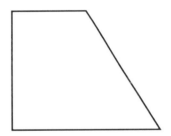

This is a Durwit.

This is a Durwit.

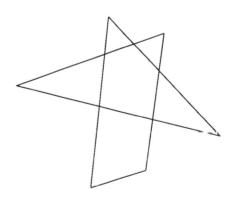

This is not a Durwit.

Kurzlas

Look at the objects in the set called Kurzlas. What attributes do they have in common that makes them members of this set? Using complete sentences, describe these attributes so that someone reading your description could name or draw a member of the same set. Keep in mind that there may be more Kurzlas than just the ones you see below. When you are finished, give the description to your partner. S/he will then name or draw a member of the set Kurzlas.

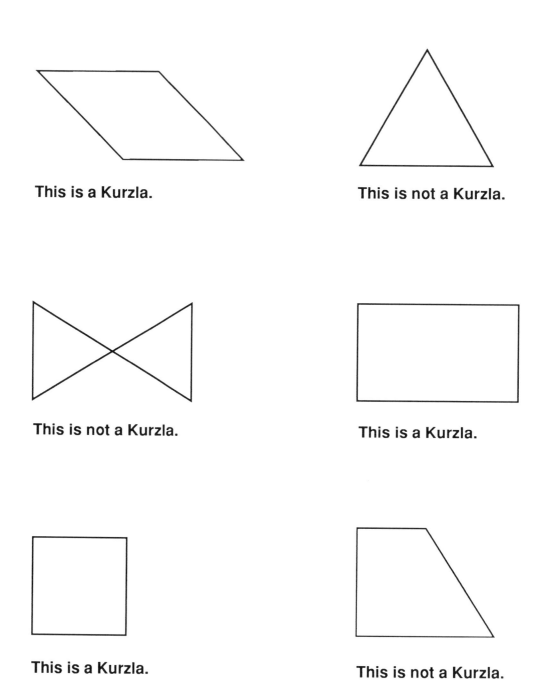

This is a Kurzla.   **This is not a Kurzla.**

This is not a Kurzla.   **This is a Kurzla.**

This is a Kurzla.   **This is not a Kurzla.**

Snigins

Look at the objects in the set called Snigins. What attributes do they have in common that makes them members of this set? Using complete sentences, describe these attributes so that someone reading your description could name or draw a member of the same set. Keep in mind that there may be more Snigins than just the ones you see below. When you are finished, give the description to your partner. S/he will then name or draw a member of the set Snigins.

A swan is a Snigin.

A cardinal is not a Snigin.

A quail is not a Snigin.

A duck is a Snigin.

A goose is a Snigin.

A heron is not a Snigin.

Edmags

Look at the objects in the set called Edmags. What attributes do they have in common that makes them members of this set? Using complete sentences, describe these attributes so that someone reading your description could name or draw a member of the same set. Keep in mind that there may be more Edmags than just the ones you see below. When you are finished, give the description to your partner. S/he will then name or draw a member of the set Edmags.

A tuna is an Edmag.　　　　　　　　**A carp is not an Edmag.**

A porpoise is not an Edmag.　　　　**A sardine is an Edmag.**

A shark is an Edmag.　　　　　　　**A rainbow trout is not an Edmag.**

Zibbers

Look at the objects in the set called Zibbers. What attributes do they have in common that makes them members of this set? Using complete sentences, describe these attributes so that someone reading your description could name or draw a member of the same set. Keep in mind that there may be more Zibbers than just the ones you see below. When you are finished, give the description to your partner. S/he will then name or draw a member of the set Zibbers.

Coal is a Zibber.　　　　　　　**Nuclear fission is not a Zibber.**

A wall plug is not a Zibber.　　**Petroleum is a Zibber.**

Methane is a Zibber.　　　　　**Smoke is not a Zibber.**

A furnace is not a Zibber.　　　**The sun is a Zibber.**

Rifers

Look at the objects in the set called Rifers. What attributes do they have in common that makes them members of this set? Using complete sentences, describe these attributes so that someone reading your description could name or draw a member of the same set. Keep in mind that there may be more Rifers than just the ones you see below. When you are finished, give the description to your partner. S/he will then name or draw a member of the set Rifers.

A kiwi is a Rifer.

A goose is not a Rifer.

A condor is not a Rifer.

An ostrich is a Rifer.

A penguin is a Rifer.

A wild turkey is not a Rifer.

Reevigs

Look at the objects in the set called Reevigs. What attributes do they have in common that makes them members of this set? Using complete sentences, describe these attributes so that someone reading your description could name or draw a member of the same set. Keep in mind that there may be more Reevigs than just the ones you see below. When you are finished, give the description to your partner. S/he will then name or draw a member of the set Reevigs.

A koala bear is a Reevig.

A kookaburra is not a Reevig.

A tree snake is not a Reevig.

A howler monkey is a Reevig.

A sloth is a Reevig.

A baboon is not a Reevig.

Dingbows

Look at the objects in the set called Dingbows. What attributes do they have in common that makes them members of this set? Using complete sentences, describe these attributes so that someone reading your description could name or draw a member of the same set. Keep in mind that there may be more Dingbows than just the ones you see below. When you are finished, give the description to your partner. S/he will then name or draw a member of the set Dingbows.

A kite is a Dingbow.   **A train is not a Dingbow.**

A car is not a Dingbow.   **A sailboat is a Dingbow.**

A glider is a Dingbow.   **A surfboard is not a Dingbow.**

Mootentootens

Look at the objects in the set called Mootentootens. What attributes do they have in common that makes them members of this set? Using complete sentences, describe these attributes so that someone reading your description could name or draw a member of the same set. Keep in mind that there may be more Mootentootens than just the ones you see below. When you are finished, give the description to your partner. S/he will then name or draw a member of the set Mootentootens.

A cat is not a Mootentooten.   **A crocodile is a Mootentooten.**

A platypus is a Mootentooten.   **A dog is not a Mootentooten.**

A snake is usually a Mootentooten.   **A spider is a Mootentooten.**

A rabbit is not a Mootentooten.   **A turtle is a Mootentooten.**

Tocktees

Look at the objects in the set called Tocktees. What attributes do they have in common that makes them members of this set? Using complete sentences, describe these attributes so that someone reading your description could name or draw a member of the same set. Keep in mind that there may be more Tocktees than just the ones you see below. When you are finished, give the description to your partner. S/he will then name or draw a member of the set Tocktees.

A ton is not a Tocktee.

A watch is a Tocktee.

An odometer is a Tocktee.

A spoon is not a Tocktee.

A scale is not a Tocktee.

A ruler is a Tocktee.

Sonar is a Tocktee.

A cup is not a Tocktee.

Gugbugs

Look at the objects in the set called Gugbugs. What attributes do they have in common that makes them members of this set? Using complete sentences, describe these attributes so that someone reading your description could name or draw a member of the same set. Keep in mind that there may be more Gugbugs than just the ones you see below. When you are finished, give the description to your partner. S/he will then name or draw a member of the set Gugbugs.

A mole is a Gugbug.

A rabbit can be a Gugbug.

A housecat is not a Gugbug.

A prairie dog is a Gugbug.

A gopher is a Gugbug.

A duck is not a Gugbug.

A monkey is not a Gugbug.

A woodchuck is a Gugbug.

Fiznors

Look at the objects in the set called Fiznors. What attributes do they have in common that makes them members of this set? Using complete sentences, describe these attributes so that someone reading your description could name or draw a member of the same set. Keep in mind that there may be more Fiznors than just the ones you see below. When you are finished, give the description to your partner. S/he will then name or draw a member of the set Fiznors.

A southwest monsoon is a Fiznor.   **A blizzard is not a Fiznor.**

A cumulus cloud is not a Fiznor.   **A typhoon is a Fiznor.**

A hurricane is a Fiznor.   **A tornado is not a Fiznor.**

Sleecos

Look at the objects in the set called Sleecos. What attributes do they have in common that makes them members of this set? Using complete sentences, describe these attributes so that someone reading your description could name or draw a member of the same set. Keep in mind that there may be more Sleecos than just the ones you see below. When you are finished, give the description to your partner. S/he will then name or draw a member of the set Sleecos.

A string bean is a Sleeco.   **An apple is not a Sleeco.**

A grapefruit is not a Sleeco.   **A cucumber is a Sleeco.**

A zucchini is a Sleeco.   **A plum is not a Sleeco.**

A cabbage is not a Sleeco.   **A peapod is a Sleeco.**

Grelcers

Look at the objects in the set called Grelcers. What attributes do they have in common that makes them members of this set? Using complete sentences, describe these attributes so that someone reading your description could name or draw a member of the same set. Keep in mind that there may be more Grelcers than just the ones you see below. When you are finished, give the description to your partner. S/he will then name or draw a member of the set Grelcers.

Larch is not a Grelcer.

Pine is a Grelcer.

Fir is a Grelcer.

Dogwood is not a Grelcer.

Holly is not a Grelcer.

Redwood is a Grelcer.

Unches

Look at the objects in the set called Unches. What attributes do they have in common that makes them members of this set? Using complete sentences, describe these attributes so that someone reading your description could name or draw a member of the same set. Keep in mind that there may be more Unches than just the ones you see below. When you are finished, give the description to your partner. S/he will then name or draw a member of the set Unches.

A carrot is an Unch.

A tomato is not an Unch.

An orange is not an Unch.

Celery is an Unch.

A radish is an Unch.

A banana is not an Unch.

An apple is an Unch.

A peach is not an Unch.

Jicama is an Unch.

Xicks

Look at the objects in the set called Xicks. What attributes do they have in common that makes them members of this set? Using complete sentences, describe these attributes so that someone reading your description could name or draw a member of the same set. Keep in mind that there may be more Xicks than just the ones you see below. When you are finished, give the description to your partner. S/he will then name or draw a member of the set Xicks.

A bird is a Xick.

A hornet is not a Xick.

An owl is not a Xick.

A butterfly is a Xick.

A bat is a Xick.

A boy is not a Xick.

Plasmoids

Look at the objects in the set called Plasmoids. What attributes do they have in common that makes them members of this set? Using complete sentences, describe these attributes so that someone reading your description could name or draw a member of the same set. Keep in mind that there may be more Plasmoids than just the ones you see below. When you are finished, give the description to your partner. S/he will then name or draw a member of the set Plasmoids.

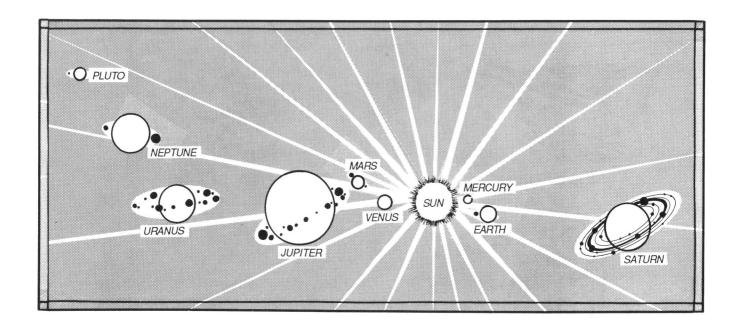

Saturn is a Plasmoid.

Neptune is not a Plasmoid.

Jupiter is a Plasmoid.

Earth is not a Plasmoid.

Uranus is a Plasmoid.

Mars is not a Plasmoid.

©1991 Midwest Publications / CRITICAL THINKING PRESS & SOFTWARE • P.O. Box 448, Pacific Grove, CA 93950

Gwigs

Look at the objects in the set called Gwigs. What attributes do they have in common that makes them members of this set? Using complete sentences, describe these attributes so that someone reading your description could name or draw a member of the same set. Keep in mind that there may be more Gwigs than just the ones you see below. When you are finished, give the description to your partner. S/he will then name or draw a member of the set Gwigs.

A lemming is not a Gwig.   **A ptarmigan is a Gwig.**

An ermine is a Gwig.   **An artic hare is a Gwig.**

A penguin is not a Gwig.   **A polar bear is not a Gwig.**

Lollies

Look at the objects in the set called Lollies. What attributes do they have in common that makes them members of this set? Using complete sentences, describe these attributes so that someone reading your description could name or draw a member of the same set. Keep in mind that there may be more Lollies than just the ones you scc bclow. When you are finished, give the description to your partner. S/he will then name or draw a member of the set Lollies.

A cup is a Lolly.   **A ruler is not a Lolly.**

A mile is not a Lolly.   **A bushel is a Lolly.**

A gallon is a Lolly.   **A fathom is not a Lolly.**

An hour is not a Lolly.   **A barrel is a Lolly.**

A liter is a Lolly.   **A pound is not a Lolly.**

A span is not a Lolly.   **A truckload is a Lolly.**

A handful is a Lolly.

Vethigs

Look at the objects in the set called Vethigs. What attributes do they have in common that makes them members of this set? Using complete sentences, describe these attributes so that someone reading your description could name or draw a member of the same set. Keep in mind that there may be more Vethigs than just the ones you see below. When you are finished, give the description to your partner. S/he will then name or draw a member of the set Vethigs.

A camel is a Vethig.

A deer is not a Vethig.

A horse is not a Vethig.

An alpaca is a Vethig.

A llama is a Vethig.

A cow is not a Vethig.

Drefs

Look at the objects in the set called Drefs. What attributes do they have in common that makes them members of this set? Using complete sentences, describe these attributes so that someone reading your description could name or draw a member of the same set. Keep in mind that there may be more Drefs than just the ones you see below. When you are finished, give the description to your partner. S/he will then name or draw a member of the set Drefs.

A flying dragon is a Dref.

A flying fox is not a Dref.

A dolphin is not a Dref.

A flying squirrel is a Dref.

A flying fish is a Dref.

A pterodactyl is not a Dref.

Prentgas

Look at the objects in the set called Prentgas. What attributes do they have in common that makes them members of this set? Using complete sentences, describe these attributes so that someone reading your description could name or draw a member of the same set. Keep in mind that there may be more Prentgas than just the ones you see below. When you are finished, give the description to your partner. S/he will then name or draw a member of the set Prentgas.

A bluebill is a Prentga.

A pelican is not a Prentga.

A flamingo is not a Prentga.

A kingfisher is a Prentga.

A bittern is a Prentga.

A spoonbill is not a Prentga.

Wirtnees

Look at the objects in the set called Wirtnees. What attributes do they have in common that makes them members of this set? Using complete sentences, describe these attributes so that someone reading your description could name or draw a member of the same set. Keep in mind that there may be more Wirtnees than just the ones you see below. When you are finished, give the description to your partner. S/he will then name or draw a member of the set Wirtnees.

Brazil is a Wirtnee.

Turkey is not a Wirtnee.

Portugal is a Wirtnee.

Kenya is not a Wirtnee.

Morocco is a Wirtnee.

Peru is not a Wirtnee.

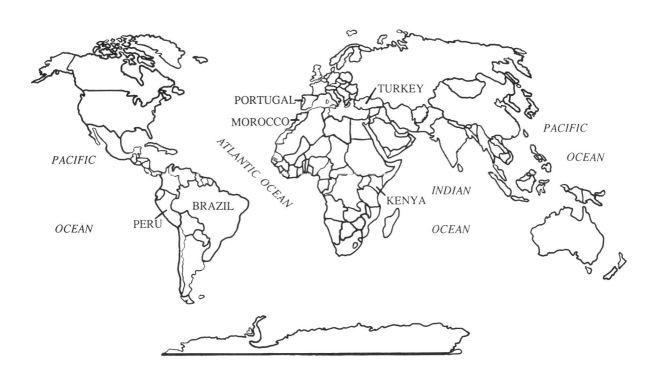

Ravsics

Look at the objects in the set called Ravsics. What attributes do they have in common that makes them members of this set? Using complete sentences, describe these attributes so that someone reading your description could name or draw a member of the same set. Keep in mind that there may be more Ravsics than just the ones you see below. When you are finished, give the description to your partner. S/he will then name or draw a member of the set Ravsics.

Canada is a Ravsic.　　　　　　　**Iceland is not a Ravsic.**

Antarctica is not a Ravsic.　　　　**Greenland is a Ravsic.**

The Soviet Union is a Ravsic.　　　**Japan is not a Ravsic.**

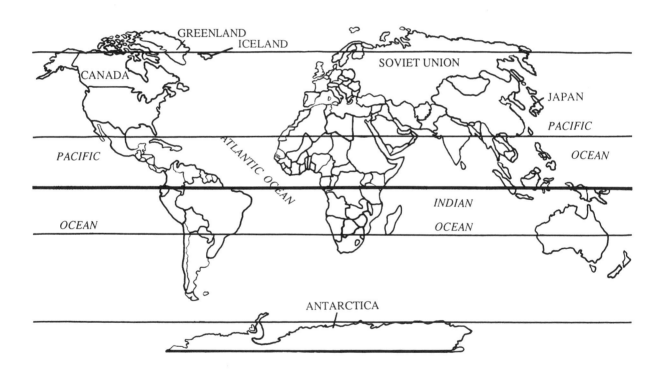

Vobers

Look at the objects in the set called Vobers. What attributes do they have in common that makes them members of this set? Using complete sentences, describe these attributes so that someone reading your description could name or draw a member of the same set. Keep in mind that there may be more Vobers than just the ones you see below. When you are finished, give the description to your partner. S/he will then name or draw a member of the set Vobers.

Egypt is a Vober.   **Syria is not a Vober.**

Libya is not a Vober.   **Sudan is a Vober.**

Uganda is a Vober.   **Chad is not a Vober.**

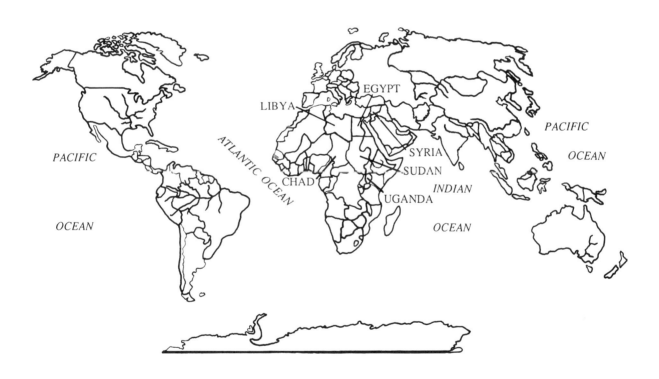

Zimmers

Look at the objects in the set called Zimmers. What attributes do they have in common that makes them members of this set? Using complete sentences, describe these attributes so that someone reading your description could name or draw a member of the same set. Keep in mind that there may be more Zimmers than just the ones you see below. When you are finished, give the description to your partner. S/he will then name or draw a member of the set Zimmers.

Antarctica is a Zimmer.   **South Africa is not a Zimmer.**

Venezuela is not a Zimmer.   **El Salvador is not a Zimmer.**

The United States is a Zimmer.   **Canada is a Zimmer.**

©1991 Midwest Publications / CRITICAL THINKING PRESS & SOFTWARE • P.O. Box 448, Pacific Grove, CA 93950